This Book Belongs To

____

Made in the USA
Coppell, TX
25 February 2023

13381798R00063